Wicked Weather

PIONEER EDITION

By Beth Geiger

CONTENTS

Wicked Weather

By Beth Geiger

Tornadoes are wicked storms. Their winds often reach 250 miles per hour. Some people risk their lives to study these deadly storms.

r

It was 6:00 p.m. on May 3, 1999. A tornado was twisting toward Oklahoma City. News reporters sent out warnings. They told people to find a safe place to hide. On a nearby highway, two trucks raced straight for the storm.

Driving Winds

That's right. The trucks sped toward the storm. Who would do that? Tornado chasers! These people study tornadoes up close.

Josh Wurman was the team's leader. He is a **meteorologist.** That is a scientist who studies weather. Wurman likes bad weather. The nastier, the better.

Double Trouble. *These two tornadoes formed side by side. Their strong winds could cause a lot of damage.*

Hit the Road

Wurman really likes tornadoes. His team drives as close to the storms as they can. Why? They want to find out when and where tornadoes form.

Wurman's trucks are weather stations on wheels. They are packed with tools. They even have **Doppler radar.** This equipment tracks storms over many miles.

Doppler radar works best when it is close to a storm. With a truck, Wurman can get the radar really close. That lets him learn a lot about tornadoes. There are many risks. But Wurman likes the challenge.

Twisted. *Circular winds twist a storm cloud. The cloud is not a tornado, but it could turn into one. Such clouds are called supercells.*

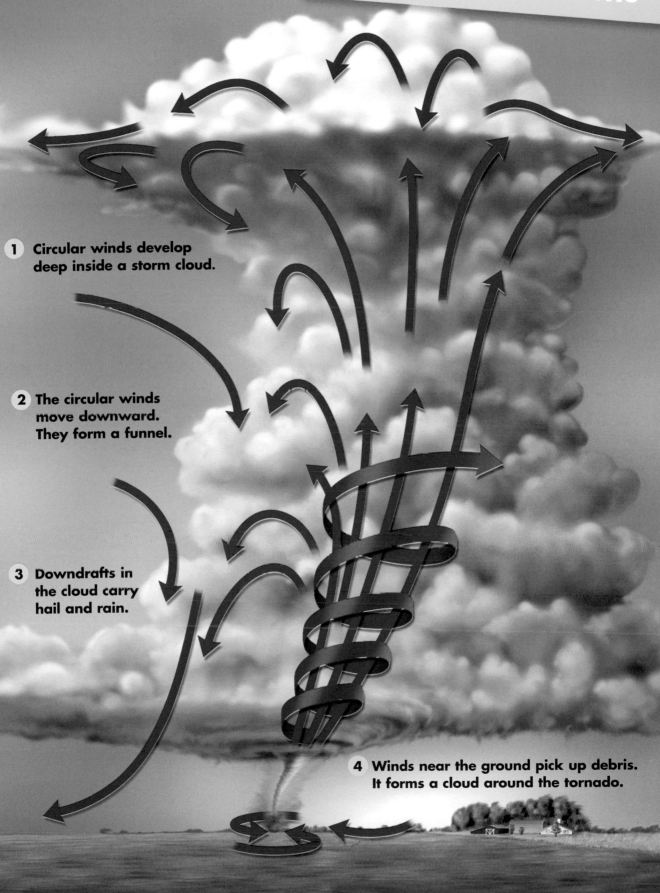

1 Circular winds develop deep inside a storm cloud.

2 The circular winds move downward. They form a funnel.

3 Downdrafts in the cloud carry hail and rain.

4 Winds near the ground pick up debris. It forms a cloud around the tornado.

Alley of Destruction. *LEFT: Most tornadoes in the U.S. form in an area called Tornado Alley. ABOVE: Tornado winds can pick up cars, trees, and almost anything else in the twister's path.*

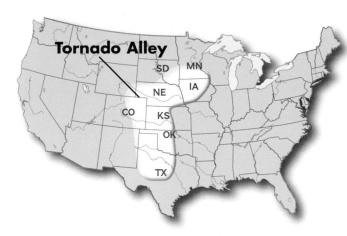

Twisted Weather

A tornado is a powerful, twisting cloud. Sometimes it is called a twister. It has a funnel. The funnel stretches down to the ground.

Tornadoes have strong winds. They can pick up houses. They can crush buildings. They can toss cars as if they were toys.

Tornado Alley

About 800 tornadoes form in the United States each year. That is more than in any other country.

Tornadoes can form anywhere at any time. Yet most form in the spring. And some places have more tornadoes than others.

Most tornadoes form in Texas, Oklahoma, Colorado, Nebraska, Kansas, South Dakota, Minnesota, and Iowa. These states are called **Tornado Alley** (see map).

Crash Course

Why do so many tornadoes form in Tornado Alley? It has to do with air. You see, warm ocean air blows over these states. Cold mountain air does too. The warm air crashes into the cold air. Then tornadoes can form. That is what happened near Oklahoma City on May 3, 1999.

Saving Lives

That day, the city made history. One tornado had winds that reached 301 miles per hour. How do we know? Wurman and his crew measured it. The tornado's winds were the fastest in history.

Wurman's job is dangerous. Yet he thinks it is worth the risks. His work could help people find out where tornadoes will form—and when. That could save many lives.

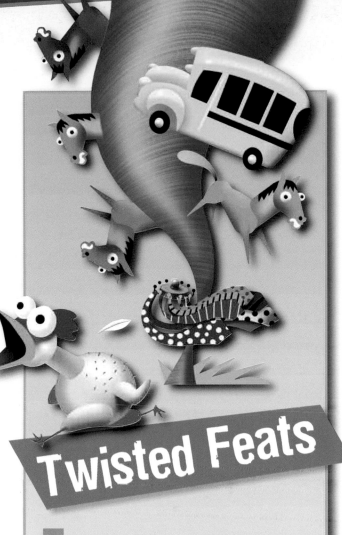

Twisted Feats

Tornadoes are known for causing a lot of damage. Yet sometimes twisters perform incredible tricks. Here are some of their fantastic feats.

November 1915 A twister picked up five horses from their barn. The tornado carried the horses a quarter mile before putting them down unharmed.

November 1915 The same tornado picked up a necktie rack with 10 ties. The rack was found 40 miles away.

June 1939 A tornado plucked the feathers off a chicken.

January 1974 A tornado picked up several empty school buses. The twister hurled the buses more than eight feet in the air.

wordwise

Doppler radar: radar system used to track storms

meteorologist: scientist who studies weather

Tornado Alley: area in the U.S. where most tornadoes form

DELMAS LEHMAN/SHUTTERSTOCK.COM (DAMAGE); NG MAPS; STEVE McCRACKEN (TORNADO ILLUSTRATION)

Tornado Ratings

Scientists rate tornadoes on a special scale. The scale measures a tornado's speed and the damage it does.

Check out the scale below. Then use it to rate each tornado described in the stories on page 9.

Measuring a Tornado

Level	Wind Speed	Damage
EF0	less than 73 mph	**Light damage:** Small tree branches broken; light poles shaken; slight damage to mobile homes and roofs of houses.
EF1	73–112 mph	**Moderate damage:** Windows broken; mobile homes pushed off their bases or flipped over; large tree branches broken.
EF2	113–157 mph	**Considerable damage:** Pieces of roof ripped off houses and other buildings; mobile homes destroyed; wooden electrical poles broken.
EF3	158–206 mph	**Severe damage:** Walls of houses, schools, and malls toppled; bark torn off trees; steel electrical poles bent or broken.
EF4	207–260 mph	**Devastating damage:** Houses destroyed; large sections of schools and malls damaged.
EF5	261–318 mph	**Incredible damage:** Schools, malls, and high-rise buildings seriously damaged or destroyed.

How big

Eyewitness Stories: Use the scale to rate each tornado.

Shaking Street Lights

I was riding in the car with my mom when the tornado hit. The winds rattled our car. A traffic light shook. It almost fell off its pole. Trash cans blew across the road. But in a few moments, the tornado was gone.

Crushing Homes

The tornado destroyed many homes in our town. It scattered cars and trucks like toys. Our apartment building is now just a pile of bricks. We are thankful to be alive.

Flying Shingles

We were in school when we heard the tornado siren. The tornado blew shingles off houses. It also knocked out the power. All the lights went out. The electrical pole outside the school had snapped in two.

Toppling Trees

The tornado hit our house. After it passed, everything was a mess. Some of our walls were crushed. The trees in our yard were bare. The storm had ripped the bark right off of them.

was it?

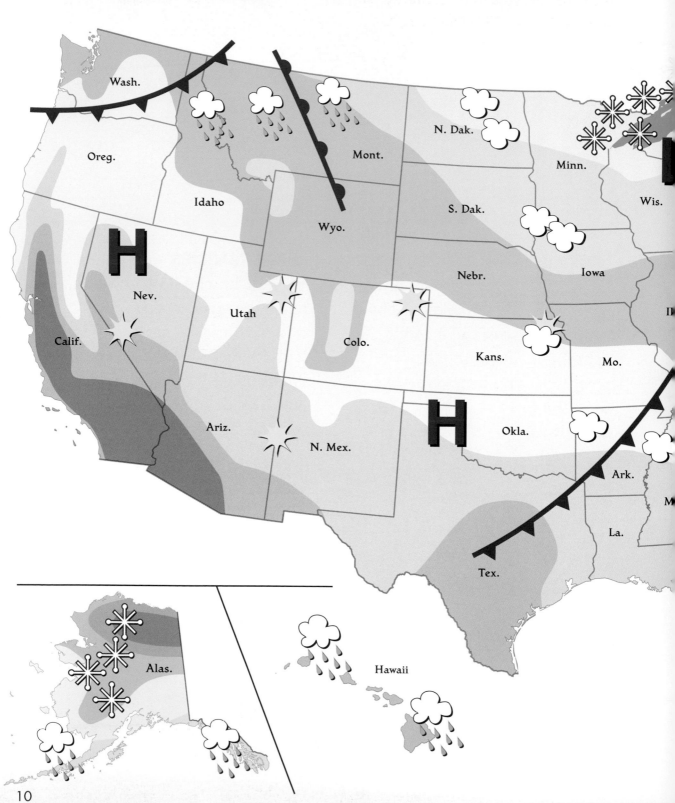

Weather maps use special symbols to show different conditions. The key tells what each symbol means. Use the key to tell what kind of weather the map shows for your state. Then pick another state. What is the weather like there?

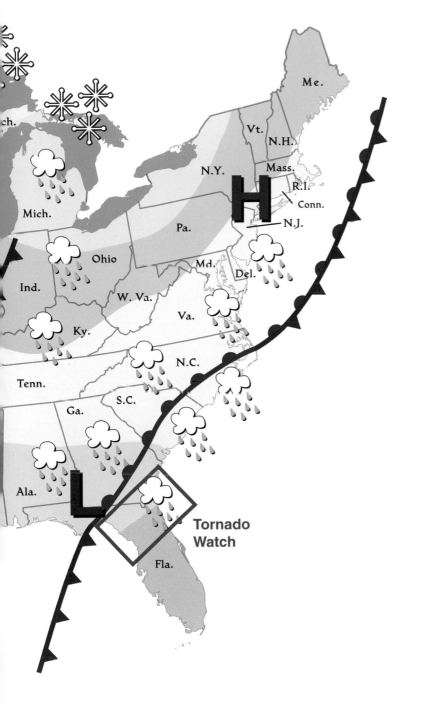

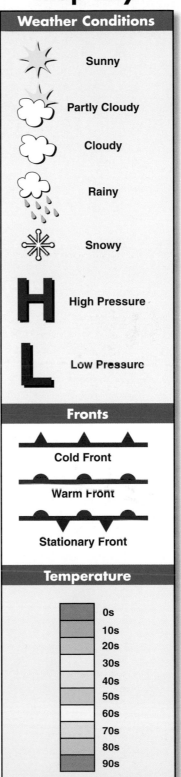

Map Key

Weather Conditions

Sunny

Partly Cloudy

Cloudy

Rainy

Snowy

H — High Pressure

L — Low Pressure

Fronts

Cold Front

Warm Front

Stationary Front

Temperature

	0s
	10s
	20s
	30s
	40s
	50s
	60s
	70s
	80s
	90s

Tornado Watch

Tornadoes

**Answer these questions to see
what you have learned.**

1 Why do tornado chasers drive
toward storms?

2 How does Doppler radar help
people study tornadoes?

3 Why are tornadoes dangerous?

4 Why do so many tornadoes
form in Tornado Alley?

5 How do scientists rate
tornadoes?